AF599008

THINK OF THAT

Holly Gardner
Art by Ilya Fortuna

CFI • An imprint of Cedar Fort, Inc. • Springville, Utah

Nephi of the Book of Mormon,
valiant in his way,
in vision saw the second coming.
He saw us in our day.

From the gathering of Israel,
willing to let God prevail,

to the building of the great city—
Zion, Zion all is well!

Joseph Smith will finish his work.
Soon the world will know
that Jesus Christ is our Savior.
Babylon He will overthrow.

President Nelson has testified
Nephi saw you and me.
He then says, "Think of that!"
It strengthens my testimony.

I wonder what I was doing
when Nephi foresaw?

I hope I was being good
and keeping God's law.

Nephi saw me.

THINK OF THAT!

I hope I was praying like Enos.

I hope I was helping like Jacob.

I hope I was repenting like Alma.

I hope I was serving like King Benjamin.

Nephi saw me.

THINK OF THAT!

I hope I was brave
like Captain Moroni.

I hope I was thankful like Sariah.

I hope I was learning like Ammon.

I hope I was righteous like Samuel.

Nephi saw me.

THINK OF THAT!

I hope I was obedient like Abinadi.

I hope I was faithful like the brother of Jared.

I hope I was a missionary like Amulek.

I hope I was writing in my journal like Mormon.

To the prophet I will listen.
I want to do my part.
Be ready to meet my Savior,
in Zion, the pure of heart.

Thank you to our beloved Prophet Russell M. Nelson who teaches truth and testifies of our Savior, Jesus Christ.

—Holly

© 2022 Holly Gardner
Illustrations © 2022 Ilya Fortuna
All rights reserved.

No part of this book may be reproduced in any form whatsoever, whether by graphic, visual, electronic, film, microfilm, tape recording, or any other means, without prior written permission of the publisher, except in the case of brief passages embodied in critical reviews and articles.

This is not an official publication of The Church of Jesus Christ of Latter-day Saints. The opinions and views expressed herein belong solely to the author and do not necessarily represent the opinions or views of Cedar Fort, Inc. Permission for the use of sources, graphics, and photos is also solely the responsibility of the author.

ISBN 13: 978-1-4621-4526-3

Published by CFI, an imprint of Cedar Fort, Inc.
2373 W. 700 S., Suite 100, Springville, UT 84663
Distributed by Cedar Fort, Inc., www.cedarfort.com

Library of Congress Control Number: 2022944737

Cover design and interior layout by Shawnda T. Craig
Cover design © 2022 Cedar Fort, Inc.

Printed in the United States of America

10 9 8 7 6 5 4 3 2 1

Printed on acid-free paper